ECHO USERS MANUAL

GET YOUR MONEY'S WORTH FROM AMAZON'S ECHO

By Steve Weber

Published by Stephen W. Weber
Printed in the United States of America
Weber Books www.WeberBooks.com
ISBN: 978-1-936560-29-5

Contents

FREE KINDLE BOOKS, ALL YOU CAN EAT! **2**

INTRODUCTION **5**

What's in the Box *6*

1 ► GETTING STARTED WITH YOUR ECHO **7**

Using Amazon's Website Instead of the Echo App *7*

If You Have Trouble During Setup *7*

Wake Up Your Echo *8*

Using Your Echo *9*

Talking to Echo *10*

Using the Remote *10*

Where to Position Echo's Body *10*

Learn How It Works by Tinkering With Echo's Flash Briefing *10*

There's Always Another Way *13*

Changing the Wake Word from "Alexa" to "Amazon" *14*

2 ► LISTENING TO MUSIC **15**

Echo Doesn't Have Your Favorite App? Don't Worry, Use Bluetooth! *16*

Using Your Echo as a Wireless Speaker via Bluetooth *17*

Accessing Your iTunes Account *18*

Using Hands-Free Playback Control for Paired Devices *18*

Cheat Sheet for Music Playback Commands *19*

Listen to Audiobooks *20*

Interrupting Alexa *20*

Silencing Alexa *21*

Say Again? *21*

3 ► AUTOMATE YOUR LIFE WITH ECHO **23**

Manage Alarms and Timers *23*

Get Weather Reports on Echo *23*

Hear Traffic Reports *24*

Adding Another Household Member's Traffic Report *24*

Manage Shopping Lists and To-Do Lists *25*

Getting Echo to Answer Questions 26
Sync Your Google Calendar with Echo 26
Re-order Items You've Bought From Amazon 27
Send Information to Kindle Fire Tablets with Voicecast 27
Enjoy Silly, Secret Echo Tricks 27
Cook Up a Recipe With IFTTT 29

4 ▶ PAIRING ECHO WITH YOUR HOME APPLIANCES **31**

The Connecting Home Devices to Echo 31
Contol a set of Home Devices 31

5 ▶ GET MORE MILEAGE FROM PRIME MUSIC **33**

Customizing Your Prime Music Experience 33
Using the Amazon Music App 34
Creating a Playlist in Your Music Library 35
Viewing Song Lyrics 35
Importing Your Own Music 36
Keeping Access to Your Music Library 36
Deleting Music From Your Library 37

6 ▶ TROUBLESHOOT YOUR ECHO **39**

Connecting With Wi-Fi. 39
Updating the Echo App 39
If Amazon Echo Doesn't Understand Your Speech 40
The Echo Remote Control Isn't Connecting 40
Can't Connect to Bluetooth 40

7 ▶ SUMMARY **43**

Introduction

Amazon has delivered a home run with the Echo, a voice-command device that plays music, answers your questions, and adds things to your grocery list just by listening to you. It's an always-on personal assistant and the first such device that's simple enough for the average consumer to begin using right away, without any technical knowledge.

Although it's a relatively small cylindrical device about the same size as two stacked soup cans, Echo delivers impressive sounds—lifelike speech and full-bodied music.

Echo is fun, useful, and a great value. Just think what it would have cost you two or three decades ago to assemble a decent home stereo—plus hundreds of dollars more for a record or tape collection! Forget that, the Echo delivers impressive sound from a collection of a million songs (through Amazon Prime) and streaming via your home Wi-Fi connection to music sites such as iTunes, Spotify and Pandora. Its pricetag is a bargain for the music function alone and new features are being added every day. And as the first generation of voice-commanded devices from Amazon, who knows what it will be able to do in a year or two's time.

Echo is the second big innovation delivered by Amazon's laboratory in Silicon Valley, following the Kindle eBook reader. The gadget runs wirelessly on the "Cloud," also known as Amazon Web Services. And that's how it's seamlessly updated with new features, as soon as they are developed by Amazon or its army of third-party software partners.

You may wonder if Amazon's Echo is just Apple's Siri in a can or Google's Now and Microsoft's Cortana, which all work with certain smartphones. Echo's Alexa may just well be another voice in the dark, but she's a sure sign that the tech giants are gearing up for computers that talk back, perform menial tasks, interface with other electronic devices, and make our lives easier and more fun.

Hopefully this book will answer all of the questions you have about the Echo. And if there's more you need to know, you can speak with an Echo product specialist at Amazon by visiting the link http://echo.amazon.com/#help/call . Type in your phone number at the site, and an Amazon rep will promptly call you back. Or just ask Alexa your question.

What's in the Box

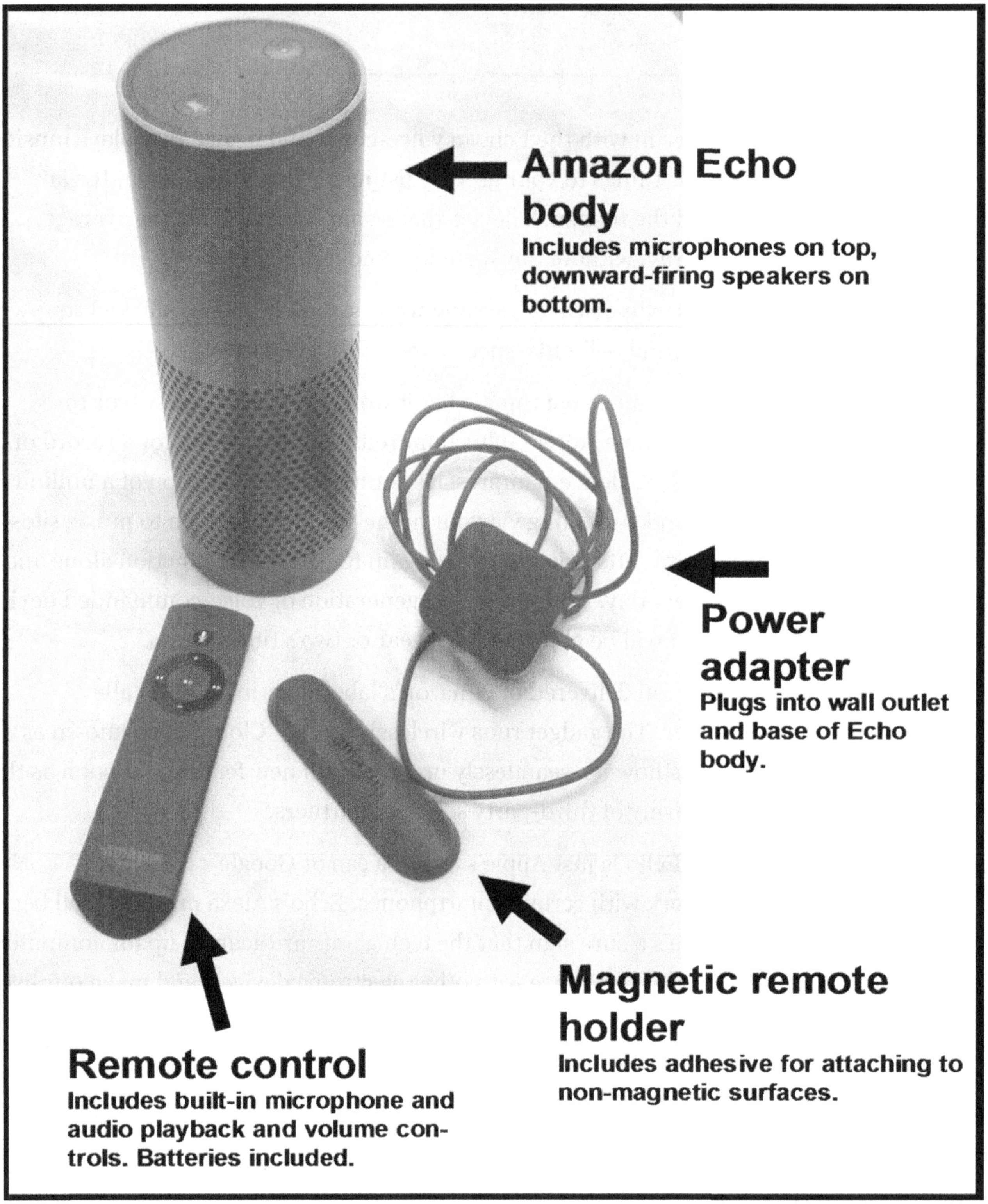

1 ► GETTING STARTED WITH YOUR ECHO

Get started by plugging your Echo into a power outlet and connecting to Wi-Fi.

1. **Plug in the Echo.** Plug the small end of the power adapter into the base of the Echo and the other end into a wall outlet. A blue light will swirl around the top edge of the Echo body. After a moment, the light should change to orange, and the Echo's voice will greet you with a "hello."
2. **Insert the two batteries into the Echo remote control.** The remote will automatically sync with the Echo body.
3. **Download the Echo app.** A free Echo application is available for smartphones and tablets. Start the download process by visiting www.amazon.com/echosetup . (There is an alternative to the Echo app—the Website interface, which we'll discuss in the next section.)

Using the app isn't mandatory for day-to-day use of your Echo, but it's essential for your Echo's initial setup and managing your lists, music, and settings.

4. **Connect Echo to a Wi-Fi network**. Launching the app will continue the setup procedure. You'll need to enter the password for your Wi-Fi network.

Using Amazon's Website Instead of the Echo App

We'll refer to Echo's app through much of this book. But sometimes you might find it easier to use Echo's Web interface using a desktop computer or laptop (especially if you have big, clumsy fingers). Open your Web browser at http://echo.amazon.com . You'll see the same navigation aids as the portable Echo app, but with more space.

If You Have Trouble During Setup

If you encounter difficulty connecting with Wi-Fi or other setup procedures, consult the "Troubleshooting" chapter at the end of this book.

Wake Up Your Echo

Your Echo is always on standby, ready to help as soon as it hears you speak the "wake word," which is "Alexa."

Let's get started. Say, "Alexa, what time is it?"

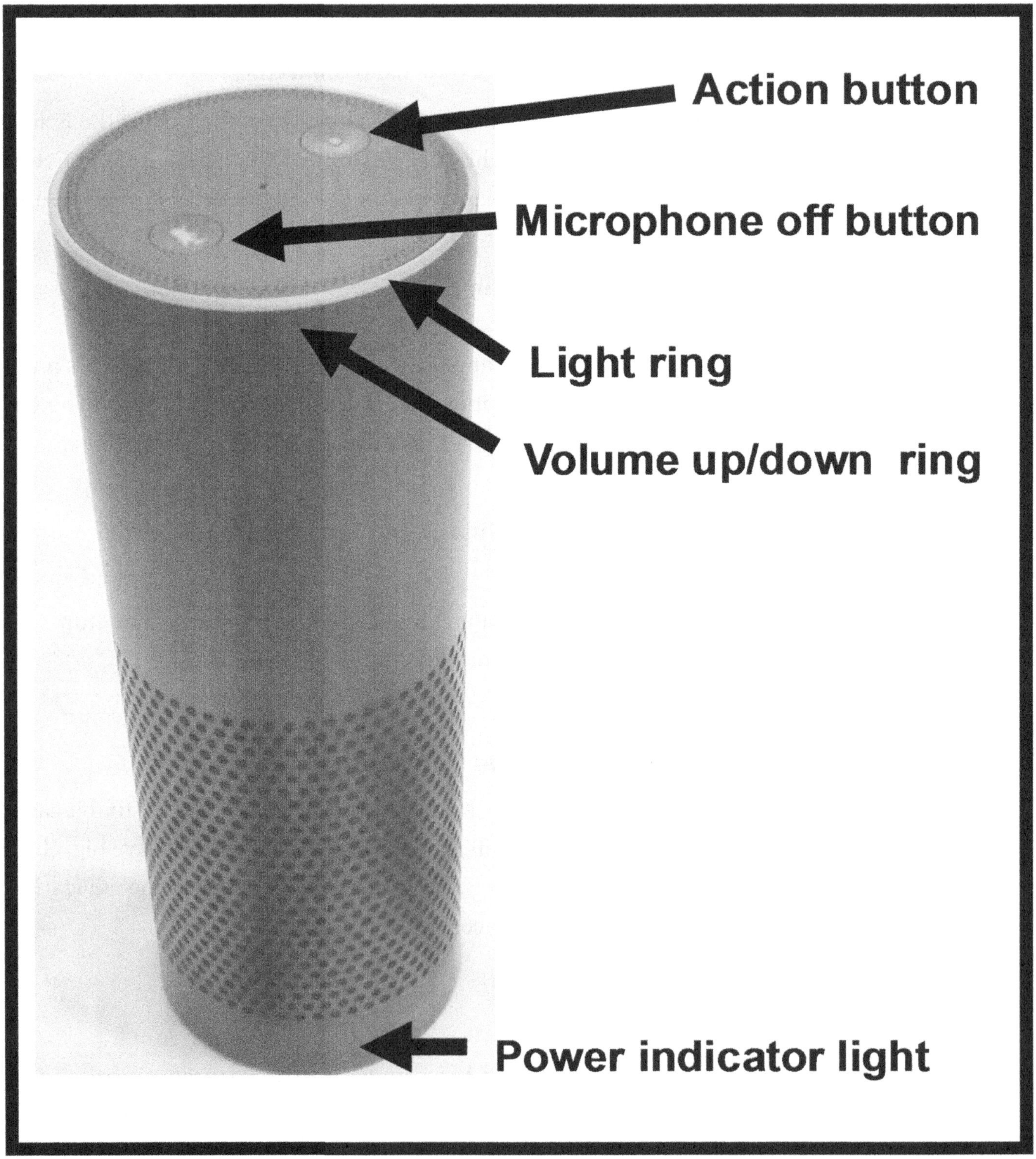

Using Your Echo

Two buttons are situated on the top of the Echo body:

Microphone button - Press this button on the top of the body to turn off Echo's microphones. The light ring will turn red, and the Echo won't hear your voice. Press the button again to turn on Echo's microphones. (While the Echo body's microphones are turned off, you can use the remote control to issue voice commands.)

Volume up/down ring - Gently grasp Echo's top edge and turn clockwise to increase the sound volume. The ring illuminates as sound is increased. Turn counter-clockwise to lower volume.

Action button - The action button on the top of the body performs three functions:

- Turns off an alarm sound or timer.
- Wakes up Echo.
- Enters Wi-Fi setup mode (press and hold the action button for five seconds).

Power light. When Echo is connected to a wall power outlet, a small white light glows at body's base. The power light indicates these statuses:

- **Solid white:** connected to Wi-Fi.
- **Solid orange:** Not connected to Wi-Fi.
- **Blinking orange:** Connected to Wi-Fi, but not connected to Amazons' Cloud.

Light ring: The color of the light ring indicates what Echo is doing. Blue indicates Echo has heard the wake-up command "Alexa" and is ready for your request. The other status indicators are:

- **Solid blue with revolving cyan lights:** Echo has been connected to a wall outlet and is starting up.
- **Solid blue with a cyan light in the direction of a person speaking:** Echo is processing your request.
- **Orange light revolving clockwise:** Echo is connecting to a Wi-Fi network.
- **White light:** Echo's volume level is being adjusted.
- **Oscillating violet light.** Echo isn't able to connect to Wi-Fi.

Talking to Echo

Echo is always on, waiting for you to say "Alexa." It is possible to change the wake word to "Amazon" but for now, everyone's Echo is named Alexa, and hopefully, your dog is not.

After waking Alexa, the light ring turns blue, and Echo awaits your request. If you're a long distance from Echo or there is lots of ambient noise, speaking into the remote control can be more effective.

Using the Remote

Press and hold the **Talk** button until you hear a beep. While the button is depressed, announce your request, then release the button. You don't need to say the "Alexa" wake word when using the remote.

The remote's playback buttons let you skip forward or back, play or pause, and adjust the volume while listening to audio.

Your remote will automatically sync with your Echo after you insert the remote's batteries.

Where to Position Echo's Body

Echo works best in a centralized location, such as on a table or countertop at least six inches away from walls and corners of a room. By not adding a built-in battery, Amazon clearly intended for Alexa to stay put on a table or counter or nightstand. But you can always move it the old fashioned way, but unplugging it here and plugging it in there.

Learn How It Works by Tinkering With Echo's Flash Briefing

Here's a great Echo feature, the Flash Briefing, and it's worth spending a few moments exploring it because it demonstrates exactly how you'll use and customize your Echo with every feature from now on.

At any time of the day or night, you can request Echo's "Flash Briefing," an up-to-the-minute summary of news, weather, and other audio items. Simply say, "**Alexa, Flash Briefing,**" and it begins. By default, the Flash Briefing begins with a news summary from National Public Radio and concludes with a weather report.

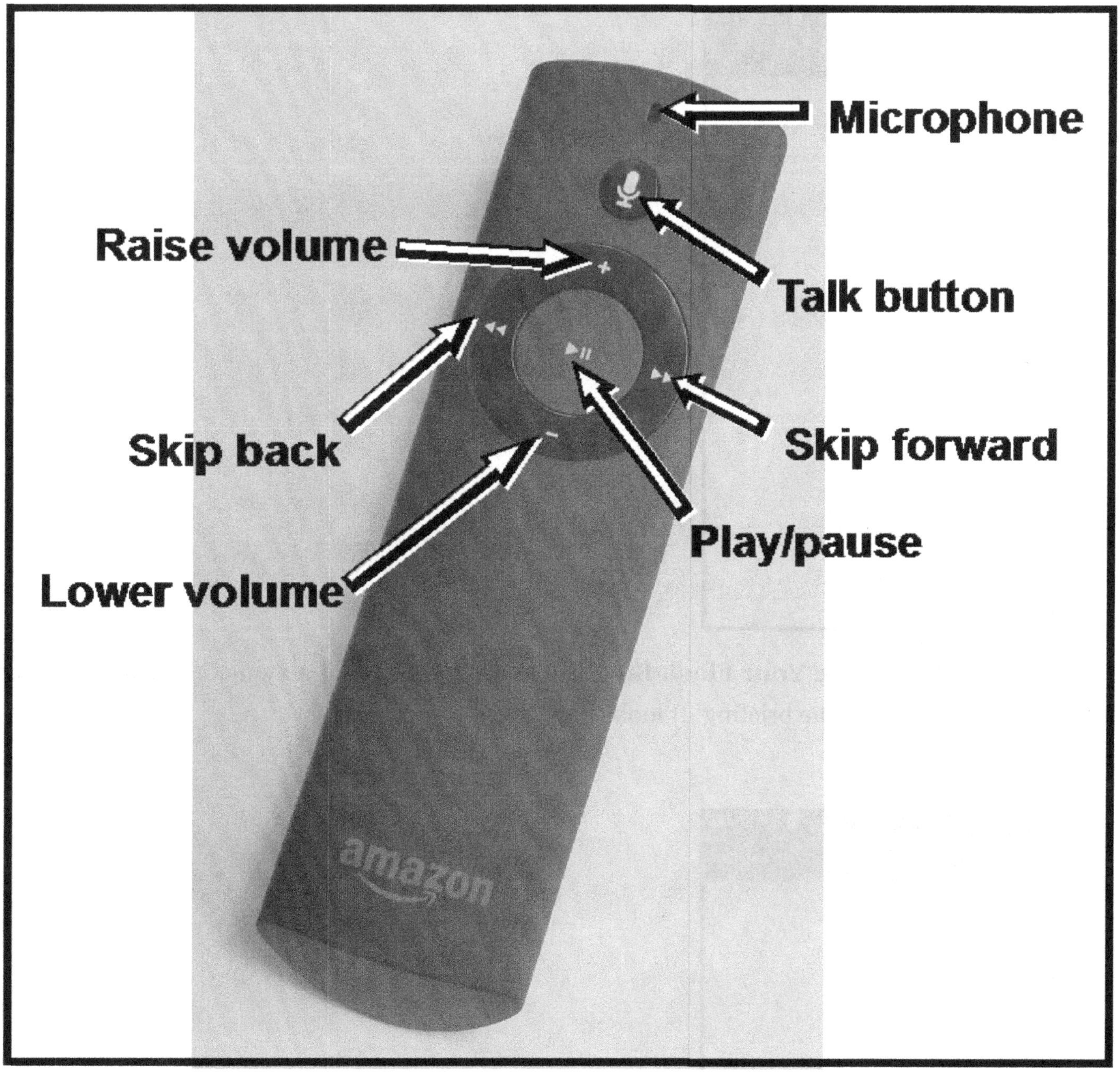

You can easily customize the Flash Briefing by deleting or adding elements within the Echo app. Let's do it:

1. Launch the Echo app on your portable device, and you'll see a "card" associated with your action of playing the Flash Briefing. (Every task you perform with the Echo generates one of these cards.) It looks like this:

2. Tap **Customize Your Flash Briefing** and you'll arrive at a menu of items you can add or delete from the briefing. It looks like this:

Toggle the switches on the right side of your screen to add or remove elements from the Flash Briefing.

That was easy, wasn't it?

There's Always Another Way

In the previous section we used the "card" in the Echo app to customize the Flash Briefing. But there's always one more way to skin a cat. Let's follow a different pathway toward changing the Flash Briefing.

1. Open the Echo app and tap the  icon at the top left corner of the home screen.
2. The navigation panel appears on the left side of your screen. It looks like this:

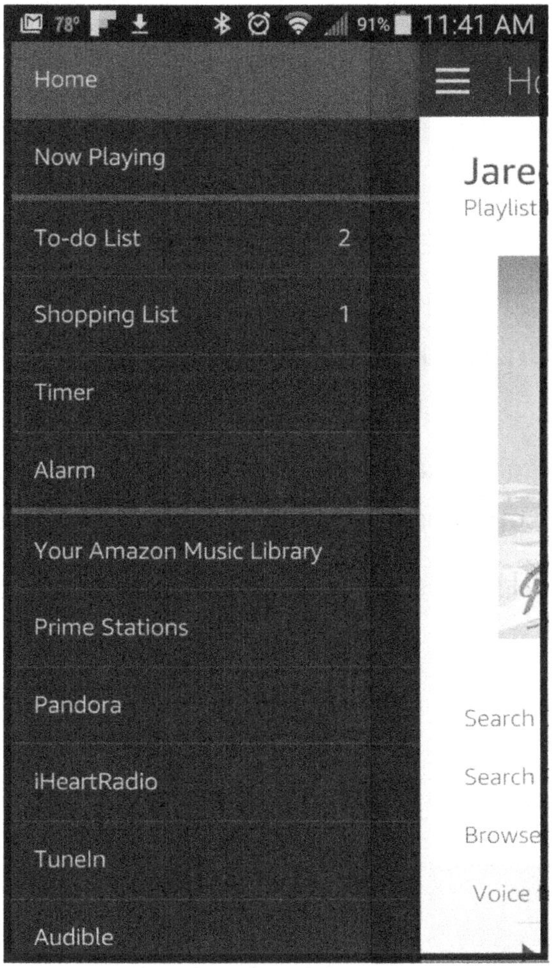

3. Scroll down the menu and tap **Settings**.

4. Scroll down and tap Flash Briefing and you'll arrive at this screen:

5. Toggle the switches on the right side of the screen to add or remove elements from your Flash Briefing.

Changing the Wake Word from "Alexa" to "Amazon"

By default, your Echo's "wake word" is "Alexa" but you can change it to "Amazon." Unfortunately, those are your only two choices. And you can't change your Echo's voice from a woman's to a man's. But who knows what Amazon has planned for software updates.

In the Echo app, go to **Settings**, select your **Echo**, and then select **Wake Word**.

2 ► LISTENING TO MUSIC

Your Amazon Echo will play music from your digital Amazon Music library, Prime Music, and other services like Spotify, Pandora, TuneIn, iHeartRadio and now iTunes. If you're not familiar with all of these services, you should take the time to give each of them a test-drive—each is quite different and offers its own special world of musical and educational content.

To begin listening to music, simply say "**Alexa, play music**" and your Echo will play a random tune from Prime Music. If you wish, you can be more specific. Instead of requesting "music," you could request a song title, artist name, playlist name, or musical genre. Or you could launch one of the separate music services described in this section, such as TuneIn, Spotify or Pandora.

Each of the following music services is supported within the Echo app. To use all of the available features—such as the ability to create personalized "radio" stations—you sometimes need to register with your email address and a password. If you already have an account with Pandora, for example, you'll be able to connect it with your Echo app.

To try out these music services, open the Echo app's left navigation panel, select **Settings > Music Services**, and tap the desired service.

Amazon Music - When you register your Echo, you automatically have access to your Amazon Music library, which includes songs and albums you've bought from Amazon. If you have digital music on your computer (or available on compact discs), you can upload that music to your Amazon Music library. You can import up to 250 songs for free, and for a fee of $25 annually the capacity grows to 250,000 songs, which is roughly the equivalent of 16,000 albums. For more information about upgrading your music storage, visit www.bit.ly/MusicStorage

Prime Music - This is Amazon's free online music, which provides access to a million songs and hundreds of playlists. Prime Music is provided free to subscribers of Amazon's Prime membership program, which also includes special shipping deals, online movies and TV shows, and other benefits. For more information, see bit.ly/amazon-prime-tunes .

TuneIn - This app brings you access to more than 100,000 local radio stations from around the world, as well as 4 million on-demand radio shows and podcasts. More details are at http://tunein.com .

iHeartRadio - This service functions as both a music recommendation system and as an aggregator of more than 800 local radio stations across the United States. iHeart has a thumbs-up/thumbs-down rating tool so you can vote on songs during their playback. Liking a song will result in it being played more often, and disliking a song will reduce its frequency. More information is at iHeartRadio.com .

Pandora - This service enables you to play preprogrammed "stations" such as "Today's Hits" or "Easy Listening" or custom stations based on a song or artist you specify. Like iHeartRadio, Pandora has a thumbs-up/thumbs-down rating tool. Liking a song will result in you hearing it more often, and a thumbs-down will ban the song from your station. Pandora also has a premium service available for $4.99 a month, which eliminates commercial interruptions and allows you to skip past unwanted songs more frequently. See Pandora.com .

Spotify - This is another service with both a free (supported by ads) and paid subscription, much like Pandora, with access to approximately 20 million songs. Users can search for artists, albums, titles, labels and genres, and create and share playlists. Spotify also includes a radio feature and has strong social media integration. See Spotify.com .

Spotify isn't supported directly in the Echo app, but you can control playback with voice commands (more on that shortly).

iTunes - Just recently Amazon announced that the Echo can access and play songs and playlists from your iTunes account. We'll tell you more about this in a minute. And to find out more about iTunes, see iTunes.com .

Echo Doesn't Have Your Favorite App? Don't Worry, Use Bluetooth!

If the Echo app is missing your favorite music service, don't fret. Virtually any content that you can play on your smartphone or tablet can be easily piped into your Echo using a nifty technology called Bluetooth. Virtually every portable digital device supports Bluetooth these days, and using it with your Echo is simple as pie. There are a couple of ways to go about it, which we'll explore in the next section.

Using Your Echo as a Wireless Speaker via Bluetooth

If you have a Bluetooth-enabled phone or tablet, you can pair it with your Echo and use the Echo as a wireless speaker. You might want to do this for a variety of reasons—perhaps you use a music app that isn't included in the Echo app. Or perhaps you want to watch a YouTube video on your cellphone while blasting the audio using your Echo. No problem, if you can play it on your mobile device, you can hear it through your Echo.

The first step in this exercise is "pairing" your mobile device with Echo using Bluetooth (this procedure only needs to be done once). Here are two methods of accomplishing the pairing:

- Using your voice:
    1. Say, **"Alexa, pair."** Your Echo should respond with the words, **"Ready to pair. Go to the Bluetooth settings on your mobile device, and choose 'Echo – [four digits]."**
    2. Open the Bluetooth settings menu on your portable device. If necessary, tap **Scan for available devices**. Select your Echo.
    3. That's it. When you're finished using the Bluetooth function, if you wish you can disconnect your portable device from the Echo's Bluetooth function. Say, "**Alexa, disconnect**."

- Using the Echo app:
    1. Select the left navigation menu, then go to **Settings**.
    2. Select your Echo's name.
    3. Tap **Bluetooth > Pairing mode**. Your Echo should respond with the words, **"Ready to pair. Go to the Bluetooth settings on your mobile device, and choose 'Echo [four digits]."**
    4. Open the Bluetooth settings on your portable device. If necessary, tap **Scan for available devices**. Select your Echo. Your Echo should respond with the words, "**Connected with Bluetooth**."
    5. When you're finished using the Bluetooth function, if you wish, you can disconnect your portable device from the Echo's Bluetooth function. Say, "**Alexa, disconnect**."

After the initial pairing, your Echo will be ready to automatically connect when you enable Bluetooth on your portable device and say, "**Alexa, connect**." If your Echo is paired with more than one portable device, it will automatically connect with the most recently connected device.

Accessing Your iTunes Account

If you want to use Echo's voice control to navigate music from iTunes, Spotify or Pandora, you must first pair it with a device that has those services. That's an upgrade from an earlier version of Echo, which only let you turn music services on and off after pairing. To do that on your phone or tablet, go to **Settings** > **Bluetooth** and say "**Alexa, pair my device.**"

With iTunes paired, for example, you can't just shout the name of your favorite band and the name of the app and start singing along. After pairing your device, select your play list on your device and the Echo will act as your device's speakers. You can then ask Alexa to **play, pause, stop, go to next, previous** or just **go back**.

If you have an Alicia Keys song on your iTunes play list, and say, "**Alexa, play Alicia Keys,**" Alexa will default to its Amazon play list. To play the song that in your iTunes library, you have to select it on your device the old-fashioned way and then let the Echo take over.

Using Hands-Free Playback Control for Paired Devices

After you've paired your portable device with your Echo, you can use hands-free voice control.

1. Say, "**Alexa, connect**." Your Echo will search for your mobile device and connect to it via Bluetooth. Your Echo will search for your device and automatically connect via Bluetooth.
2. While playing audio on your portable device while listening through your Echo, you can use these voice commands:

- Play
- Pause
- Previous
- Next
- Stop
- Resume

- Restart

During Bluetooth-connected playback, if you use your voice to request playback of a song in your Amazon Music library, your Echo will disconnect from your mobile device and Bluetooth playback will be paused. To resume, say "Alexa, connect" and select **Play** on your mobile device.

Hands-free playback doesn't work with Mac OSX devices like MacBook Airs.

Cheat Sheet for Music Playback Commands

You might never need to use all of these various commands for controlling Echo's audio playback. But here they are anyway:

- Adjusting the volume

Say, **"Alexa, turn the volume up [or down]."** Or say, **"Alexa, Volume [1 through 10]."**

Or using Echo App: Tap the ☰ icon, then tap **Now Playing.** Touch the **Volume** icon at the bottom of the screen and slide it up or down.

- Get information about music being played

Say, **"Alexa, what song [or who] is this?"**

Or using the app: Tap **Now Playing** and view the details.

- Stop track being played

Say, **"Alexa, Stop [or Pause]."**

Or using the app: Tap the **Pause** icon.

- Play song

Say, **"Alexa, Play [or Resume]."**

Or using the app: Tap the **Play** icon.

- Skip to next or previous track

Say, **"Alexa, Next [or Previous]"** or **"Alexa, go back."**

Or using the app: Tap the **Next** or **Previous** icon.

- Shuffle songs (or alternatively, play songs in the album's original sequence)

Say, **"Alexa, Shuffle [or Stop Shuffle/Shuffle Off]."**

Or using the app: Select the **Shuffle** icon.

Listen to Audiobooks

If you have an account at Audible.com, your audiobooks will automatically show up in your Echo app. From the home screen, tap the ☰ icon. Scroll down and tap **Audible**. You'll see a list of your audiobooks.

You can control audiobook playback by using the app, as well as voice commands:

- Listen to an Audiobook.

Say, **"Alexa, play the audiobook [Title]."**

Or using the app: Tap the ☰ icon, scroll down and tap **Audible**. Select the desired title.

- Skip Forward or Reverse by 30 Seconds

Say, **"Alexa, go back [or forward]."**

Or using the app: Open the **Now Playing** bar and select the **Go Back** or Go **Forward** icon.

Echo also supports **Whispersync for Voice**, which remembers your most recent playback position in your audiobooks. So, for example, you can begin listening to an audiobook on your Kindle Fire tablet, then resume the audiobook on the Echo without losing your place.

Interrupting Alexa

If you ask Alexa to play music from your favorite radio station and then ask her about the weather, the music will fade as she tells you about the rain heading your way. To get back to the music, you'll may need to ask her to play your favorite radio station again, which probably has more to do with the steadfastness of your Internet conncetion than anything else. Otherwise, the music returns.

As you remember to take that umbrella when you go out, we hope you remember to shut off the music, just to be green.

Silencing Alexa

If you want Alexa to go completely silent for a while or whatever reason, there's a mute button on the top of the can. Press it and a red ring will appear and Alexa will stay mute until you press the button again.

Say Again?

If you didn't hear Alexa's answer to a question, maybe because the phone rang or your dog barked, Alexa is happy to repeat it. Simply say, **"Alexa, can you repeat that?"** and she will. For some reason, "repeat that" alone doesn't seem to work as well as "can you repeat that."

3 ► AUTOMATE YOUR LIFE WITH ECHO

There are dozens of ways to automate your life by using the Echo app or voice commands, and more are constantly being added.

Manage Alarms and Timers

You can use one alarm and one countdown timer on Echo, and each can be set up to 24 hours ahead.

- To set an alarm

Say, **"Alexa, wake me up at [time]."**

Or say, **"Alexa, set the alarm for [x minutes/hours] from now."**

Or using the app: Open the left navigation panel and select **Alarm**. Select a time and tap **On**.

- To Cancel an Alarm

Say, **"Alexa, cancel the alarm."**

Or say, **"Alexa, stop the alarm."**

- Snooze alarm

Say, "**Alexa, snooze**." The alarm will go silent, then resume after nine minutes.

Your alarm and timer will sound even if Echo is muted. You can adjust the timer or alarm volume by adjusting the **Device Settings** in the Echo app.

Get Weather Reports on Echo

After you specify your Zip Code in the Echo app, you can ask for local weather reports, conditions, and forecasts for the next seven days. Weather information is updated every 30 minutes by Accuweather, and you can access information on any U.S. or foreign city.

For current local weather: "Alexa, what's the weather?"

For local forecasts: "Alexa, what's the weather for this [weekend/day of the week]?"

For future conditions: "Alexa, will it snow tomorrow?"

For weather for a different city: "Alexa what's the weather in [city/country]?"

Hear Traffic Reports

You can add your commute details to the Echo app, then ask Echo for traffic conditions on your route. Echo will recommend the best route and estimated commute time for the current conditions.

1. From the Echo app, open the left navigation panel and tap **Settings**.
2. Select **Traffic**.
3. In the **From** and **To** fields, select **Change address**. Enter a starting point and destination address in both sections. You can also enter a "stop" along the way.
4. Enter a new address or select one from your Amazon account, then select **Save Changes**.

To get a traffic report, say, "Alexa, how is traffic?"

Adding Another Household Member's Traffic Report

If you and your partner go in separate directions, you can progam your Echo to give a separate traffic report. Your partner, however, needs to have his or her own Amazon account and will need to be present to log into it.

1. Open to the Echo app for the primary Echo account holder—this would be the person under whose account the Echo was originally ordered.

2. Tap **Settings**, then tap the **Household Profile**.

3. Follow the on-screen prompts to add the second Amazon account holder to your Household.

Now the person you've added needs to download and install the Echo app on his or her phone, and enter their own commute details in the app's Traffic screen.

With your Household set up, each of you has a separate Echo "profile." To toggle between then, say, **"Alexa, switch profiles."** The Echo will switch profiles and tell you which profile is now active.

To learn which profile is active, say, "**Alexa, current profile**," or, "**Alexa, whose profile**."

To access each person's Traffic Report, just switch to the profile of the Household member whose Traffic Report is wanted, then use the regular Traffic Report commands to hear it.

Two Profiles

Setting up separate profiles also allows the two different household members to access their separate content via the Echo, such as their separate Amazone music accounts, separate iHeart Radio, Pandora, iTunes and so on, and separate Amazon one-click shopping accounts.

Manage Shopping Lists and To-Do Lists

You can view up to 100 items on your Shopping or To-Do Lists using the Echo app. If you're using the Echo app on your computer, you can print the lists.

Using voice commands: Say, **"Alexa, add [item] to my Shopping/To-Do List."**

Using the app: Select **Shopping List** or **To-Do List** in the left navigation panel. Enter the name of the item in the text field and select the + icon. Each item in your list can be as many as 250 characters long. Remember, too, that most devices (phone, tablet) have a "dictate" mode on your keyboard so you are able to speak the names of the items you want added to your list. But alas, that's what Alexa is for.

You can delete items from your lists by using the Echo app. **Select Shopping List** or **To-Do List** in the left navigation panel. Select the downward arrow next to the item you want to delete and select **Delete item**.

To edit items in your lists, select an item in the list touch the pen tools to edit the item, make your change, then select **Save**.

To search Amazon for an item on your list, select the item, then select **Search Amazon for**....

Getting Echo to Answer Questions

Echo will retrieve information from public resources such as Wikipedia to answer questions. For example, try saying, "**Alexa, who is Abraham Lincoln**?" Echo will read the first paragraph from the introduction of the Wikipedia entry for Lincoln. You can get a bit more than the first paragraph if you say, "**Alexa, More**." But Echo won't read the entire Wikipedia article.

Here are some examples of the type of information Echo will retrieve for you:

People: "Alexa, who is [name]?"

Dates: "Alexa, when is [holiday]?"

Films: "Alexa, who starred in [movie title]?"

Music: "Alexa, who sings the song [song title]?"

Spelling: "Alexa, how do you spell [word]?"

Definitions: "Alexa, what is the definition of [word]?"

Conversion/Measurements: "Alexa, how many [units] are in a [unit]?"

Arithmetic: "Alexa, what is [number] times [number]?"

Geography: "Alexa, what is the capital of [location]?"

Echo will also retrieve sports scores and schedules about professional and college basketball, professional football, and professional hockey and soccer games and teams.

You can also ask miscellaneous items, such as "**Alexa, tell me a joke**."

Sync Your Google Calendar with Echo

If you don't already have a Google calendar, you can create one at https://calendar.google.com .

1. From the Echo app's left navigation panel, select **Settings > Calendar Services**.
2. Select **Link account on Google**.
3. Enter your Google e-mail address and password, then follow the instructions to access your calendar. Then you can use these voice commands:

"Alexa when is my next event?"

"Alexa, what's on my calendar?"

"Alexa, what's on my calendar tomorrow?"

Re-order Items You've Bought From Amazon

To place an order, say "**Alexa, reorder [item name].**" Echo will confirm the item name and cost, then Alexa will will ask if you want to go ahead and order it. You can say, "Yes," and the item is ordered just like clicking the "Buy Now With One Click" button on the Amazon site.

If it's the first time and you're hesitant to pull the trigger, just say, "No," and check the Echo app. It will show additional details about the item and your "ship to" address. If you click on the card, the app and it will take you directly to the Amazon order page, showing other vendors for the item.

If the item is out of stock, Echo will try to find an alternative item and retrieve details.

Send Information to Kindle Fire Tablets with Voicecast

Using Echo's Voicecast feature, you can send information about you've heard through Echo to your Kindle Fire tablet. This works with information regarding music, Wikipedia, Questions and Answers, Flash Briefing, To-Do Lists and Shopping Lists, Weather, Time & Alarms, and Help.

1. To turn on Voicecast, open the Echo app's left navigation panel, then select **Settings**.
2. Select **Voicecast**, then use the switch to turn it on.

If you want Echo-retrieved information to appear on your tablet, say, **"Alexa, show this on my [name of device].**

Enjoy Silly, Secret Echo Tricks

Part of the fun you can have with your Echo is probing for "secret" features that haven't been publicized by Amazon. Here are some humorous features as compiled by David Lari, a software developer who blogs at bit.ly/silly-echo-tricks .

Try asking your Echo David's questions, and you'll likely be amused:

- Alexa, tell me a joke.
- Alexa, what is love?

- Alexa, what is the meaning of life?
- Alexa, who is better, you or Siri?
- Alexa, what does the fox say? (Repeat for different answers.)
- Alexa, live long and prosper. (Repeat for different answers.)

You can prompt your Echo with quotes from famous movies and see if they're recognized, such as these:

- From 2001 A Space Odyssey: "Alexa, open the pod bay doors."
- From Jerry McGuire: "Alexa, show me the money!"
- From Wayne's World: "Alexa, party on, Wayne."
- From Airplane: "Alexa, Surely, you can't be serious."
- From The Princess Bride: "Alexa, my name is Inigo Montoya."
- From A Few Good Men: "Alexa, I want the truth."

Want more? Here's part of another compilation archived at the Reddit website: bit.ly/more-echo-tricks :

- Alexa, beam me up.
- Alexa, how much wood can a woodchuck chuck if a woodchuck could chuck wood?
- Alexa, define supercalifragilisticexpialodocious.
- Alexa, who's your daddy?
- Alexa, Earl Grey. Hot. (or Tea. Earl Grey. Hot.)
- Alexa, what does the Earth weigh?
- Alexa, when is the end of the world?
- Alexa, is there a Santa?
- Alexa, make me a sandwich.

Is It Christmas Yet?

Alexa celebrates a few holidays and can tell you how many days until Christmas or when Labor Day is. She fails, however, to know when Yom Kippur falls but does know about Easter and Halloween. She's also short on sports and doesn't know when the Super Bowl will be played.

Simon Says

You can have fun with your family, especially little kids, when you use the remote control from another room and have Echo say fun things. Kids will think Echo is talking directly to them.

To make Echo say whatever you want, say, **"Alexa, Simon says ..."** followed by what you want to say. Alexa is programmed to bleep profanity (yes, we tried).

Cook Up a Recipe With IFTTT

Okay, we're getting geeky now. We're talking about recipes, but not the food kind. We're going to use IFTTT, which stands for "If This, Then That." It's a service that connects your favorite devices, apps, and websites with simple rules called "recipes." For example, you can design a recipe that allows Echo to find your phone or even print your shopping list

IFTTT is limited only by your imagination. Amazon's most recent update allows you to trigger action for specific sports scores and schedules and to share a song to Facebook and Twitter.

Let's explore one example—using Echo to find your smartphone.

On your computer or phone, open the Web link https://ifttt.com/recipes/288400-find-your-phone-by-asking-alexa . (Here's a shorter version of the link: bit.ly/find-phone-echo).

You'll be prompted to register an account with IFTTT, and you'll receive a confirmation email you must click before you can use the service.

Ready? Now ask, "**Alexa, what's on my To-Do list?**" You'll hear the items on your list, and your phone will ring.

You can make up your own recipies or use one of the "shared" creations listed at https://ifttt.com/amazon_alexa . Some of the most popular:

- Add Echo's To-Do list to Google Calendar.

- E-mail your Shopping List to yourself when you ask Alexa what's on your list.
- Add your Alexa To-Do's to Evernote.

Amazon just announced some enhanced IFTTT features, such as a social media sharing component. **IF** you ask Alexa for a song, **THEN** the song can be shared on Facebook or Twitter.

4 ► PAIRING ECHO WITH YOUR HOME APPLIANCES

Amazon will, undoubtedly, keep rolling out updates for the Echo that increase its functionality. The latest update adds support for WeMo and Hue devices. This enables users to control lighting and electrical devices in the home by voice.

The Connecting Home Devices to Echo

If you have a "smart" home device such as a light strip or appliance switch, you can control it with your Echo. For example, you'd be able to turn off your bedroom lights after you're under the covers without clapping on and clapping off.

For a list of compatible devices, consult the Amazon Help page, bit.ly/echo-devices . Only a few are available now but no doubt, more are on their way. Echo currently supports:

- WeMo: Switch, Insight Switch, and Light Switch
- Hue: A19, Lux, BR30, Bloom, and LightStrip Lights

After installing a supported device, such as a light switch, say, **"Alexa discover my appliances."** From that point on, Alexa can turn on and off the lights. According to Amazon, some of these commands will turn your home into a smart home.

- Alexa, turn on the hallway light."
- Alexa, turn on the coffee maker."
- Alexa, dim the light by 50%."
- Alexa, turn off the outdoor holiday lights."

Contol a set of Home Devices

If you want to control a group of devices, such as three lights in your office, you need to set it up as a group and name it. And if you can't remember the name of your group (desk lamps versus desk lights), set up two groups, one with each name to control the same devices. This also works for two profiles where you can group three lights and your partner can group two.

5 ▶ GET MORE MILEAGE FROM PRIME MUSIC

If you're just starting to dabble with Amazon's music service, this chapter will serve as a roadmap for getting the most out of it. If you've ever used a streaming music service like Pandora, Spotify, or Rhapsody, you'll be glad to know that Prime Music is included in your Prime subscription and provides more than a million songs, along with hundreds of playlists. (A playlist is a list of songs that can be played in sequential or random order.) You can enjoy the service free without commercial interruptions.

Prime Music is like a personalized radio station—the more you use it, the better it gets because it learns your musical preferences. You can easily rate songs with a thumbs-up (if you like it) or thumbs-down (if you hate it), and this fine-tunes the music you'll hear later.

You can start listening to Prime Music by saying, **"Alexa, play Prime Music."** Or within the Echo app, open the left navigation panel and select **Prime Stations**. Or to access Prime Playlists, select **Your Amazon Music Library**, then **Playlists**. Scroll down to **Prime Playlists**. You'll find the usual country, '60s Rock, and Jazz, but you'll also see playlists for artists such as Justin Timberlake, Louis Armstrong, and Beethoven. You can search by **Genre** or **Artist A-Z.** Try asking Alexa to play "dinner music" or "music to study by."

Customizing Your Prime Music Experience

Prime Music lets you rate songs by voting thumbs-up or thumbs-down whenver you wish. To rate a song while you're listening to a Prime Station using the Echo app, tap on the panel at the bottom of your screen showing the artist and song title. Thumbs-up and thumbs-down icons will appear.

You can listen to Prime Music on Kindle Fire tablets, Apple and Android tablets and smartphones, PC and Mac computers, and using Amazon's Prime Music Library on the Web player, located at bit.ly/MusicCloudPlayer .

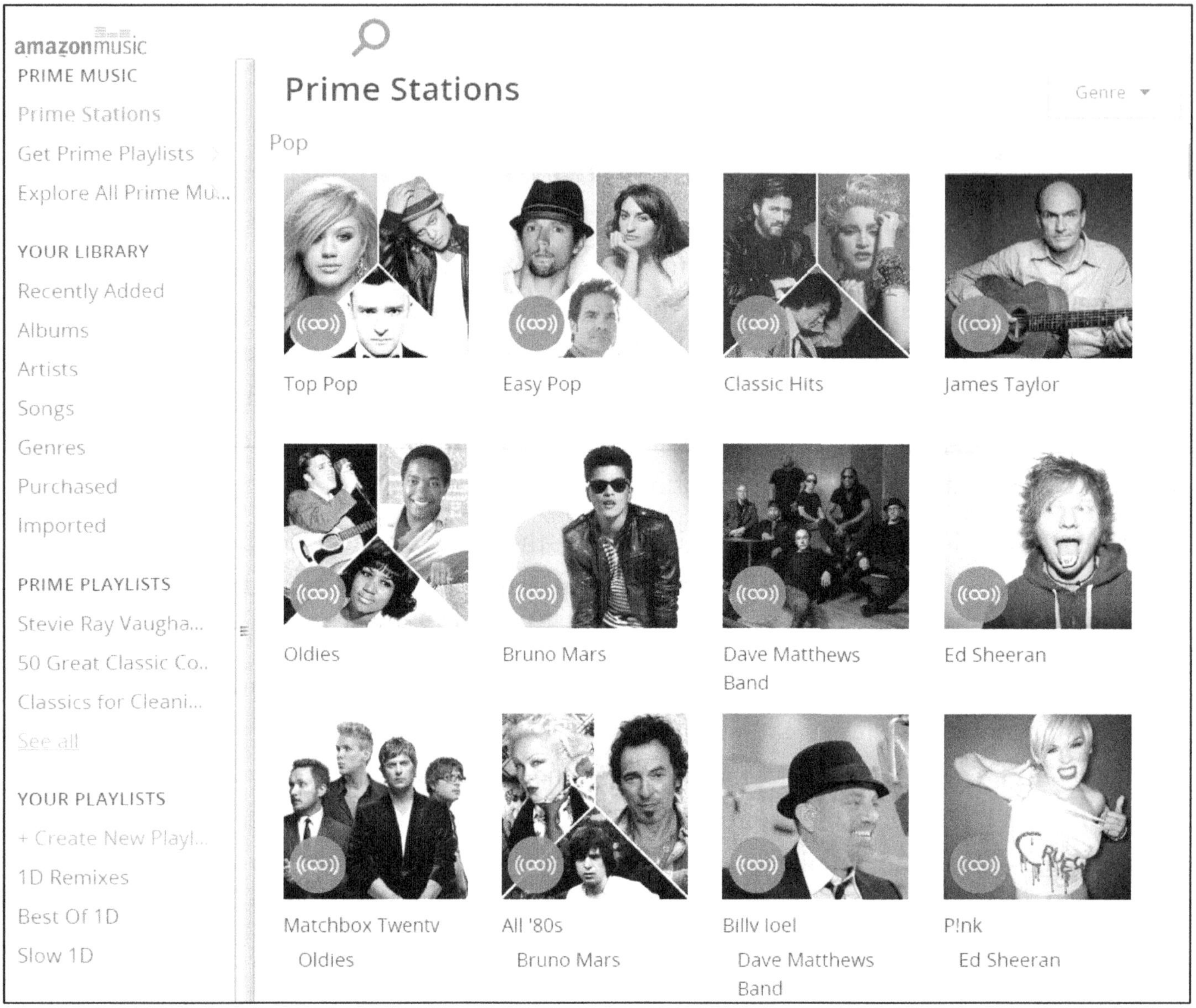

Above: A view of Prime Music Library on the Web player, https://www.amazon.com/gp/dmusic/cloudplayer/web

Another big plus with Prime Music is your unlimited ability to skip past songs you don't want to hear—some competing services only allow you to skip over a few unwanted songs per hour.

Using the Amazon Music App

If you use a mobile device to listen to music, you might be interested in test-driving the Amazon Music app available in the Amazon Appstore, Google Play, and Apple's appstore. Search the appstore for "Amazon Music" then follow the instructions on your screen to install the app and sign in with your Amazon account. After you've installed the music app, swipe from the left edge of your screen or tap the **Menu** button to access your library.

The big advantage of the Amazon Music app compared to the Echo app is that the Music App is truly portable—for example, you can use it while driving, streaming the audio to your car stereo using Bluetooth. By contrast, with the Echo app, you're restricted to locations where your Echo can reach a power outlet and Wi-Fi.

If you prefer using the Amazon Music app, you can connect it with your Echo by using Bluetooth. Consult the previous chapter, "Listening to Music," and the section "Using your Echo as a wireless speaker using Bluetooth."

For more information about the Amazon music app and links to the versions for different types of devices, visit the page bit.ly/AmazonMusicApps .

Creating a Playlist in Your Music Library

To create a playlist in your music library using the Amazon Music app:

1. Visit the Playlists section and tap **+Create New Playlist**. (On Kindle Fire tablet, it's simply a + icon.
2. Enter a name for your playlist and tap **Save**.
3. Select the songs you want added to your playlist.
   - On the Web, click **Add to playlist**, then select playlist name from the drop-down menu.
   - Using the Amazon Music App, select **Done**.

Viewing Song Lyrics

You can view lyrics for many Prime songs while listening to music on your Kindle Fire tablet or Amazon Music app for Android or Apple. Eligible songs have a **Lyrics** label next to the title, and an **X-Ray** or **Lyrics** panel on the Now Playing screen.

Lyrics display line-by-line, synchronized with the playback. You can tap or drag the lyrics panel to expand or hide the lyrics.

To view lyrics on Amazon Music for PC or Mac, click the album icon or the lyrics badge next to the playback controls.

Importing Your Own Music

If you already have a personal collection of music, you can use the **Amazon Music Importer** on your computer to add that music to your library, so you can play it from all your connected devices.

To import:

Visit your music library, https://www.amazon.com/musiclibrary using your computer.

On the left menu, click **Upload Your Music**. If you're prompted to install the Importer, follow the instructions on your computer screen.

After you've opened or installed Amazon Music Importer, click **Start Scan** to search your iTunes and Windows Media Player libraries for songs available for importing. To search elsewhere on your computer, click **Browse Manually**, which can take quite a while.

After the Importer has located your music, click **Import All** to add all the files to your library. Or click **Select Music** to identify which songs you want to add.

Amazon allows you to import up to 250 songs at no cost. With an Amazon Music subscription costing $24.99 annually, you can import as many as 250,000 songs. For more information, visit

Amazon's **Manage Your Cloud Subscription** page, https://www.amazon.com/clouddrive/manage .

Keeping Access to Your Music Library

There are a few scenarios in which you won't have access to your Prime music. First, the selection of available Prime music changes continuously—new titles are constantly added, while some are dropped. Discontinued titles will remain listed in your library, but are greyed out and can't be played. To regain access to those titles, you'd need to purchase them from Amazon.

Secondly, if your Amazon Prime membership expires, you will no longer have access to the Prime music you've added to your library.

Thirdly, music you've downloaded to your mobile device through the Amazon Music app won't be immediately available if you haven't used the app while connected to the Internet for the past 30 days. In that case it may take about 10 minutes for you to regain access to the downloaded music after you reconnect with the app.

And finally, Prime music you've downloaded for playback offline is deleted from your device if you sign out of the Amazon music app.

Sometimes, if you can't find the music you're looking for, you merely need to refresh your library. Open the app menu (swipe from the left edge of the screen or tap the **Menu** button), select **Settings**, then select **Refresh** at the top of the screen.

Deleting Music From Your Library

You can delete music files from your library using a Web browser on your computer.

Visit your music library, https://www.amazon.com/musiclibrary .

Check the boxes next to each file you want to delete.

Select multiple songs by checking the box next to the first song to be deleted, press and hold the **Shift** key on your keyboard, then check the box beside the last song to be deleted. This highlights all songs between the top and bottom song selected.

6 ► TROUBLESHOOT YOUR ECHO

The following tips will help you resolve the most common issues related to the Amazon Echo and its app. If you still have trouble, and if there's more you need to know, you can speak with an Echo product specialist at Amazon by visiting the link http://echo.amazon.com/#help/call . Type in your phone number at the site, and an Amazon rep will promptly call you back.

Connecting With Wi-Fi.

Echo requires a Wi-Fi connection to hear your commands, talk back to you, and play music stored in Amazon's Cloud.

1. Plug Echo into a wall power outlet and open the Echo App on your phone, tablet, or computer. If necessary, download the app from www.amazon.com/echosetup .
2. In the Echo app, open the navigation panel on the left. Select **Settings > [Your Name]'s Echo > Update Wi-Fi**. If you're adding a new Echo to your account or setting up your Echo for the first time, select **Set up a new Echo**.
3. Press and hold the **Action** button on the top of your Echo's body, holding the button for five seconds. The light ring becomes orange, and your tablet, phone or computer connects with Echo. A list of nearby Wi-Fi networks is shown in the app.
4. Select your Wi-Fi's name, enter the password, and select **Connect**. If you can't find the name of your network, scroll down and select **Rescan** or Add a **Network**.

After your Echo connects to Wi-Fi, a confirmation message appears in the app. Return to the app's Home screen to begin using Echo.

Note that if you move your Echo around, say between your office and your home, once you have set up a Wi-Fi connection, the Echo will automattically log into that Wi-Fi again without having to set it up and enter a password each time it's moved.

Updating the Echo App

Periodically Amazon adds new features and services to the Echo app. Every couple of months, you should search for an update by visiting the app store on your device and search for "Amazon Echo." When an update is available, tap the **Update** button to install it. If an update button isn't visible, you have the latest version of the Echo app.

If Amazon Echo Doesn't Understand Your Speech

When issuing voice commands to your Echo, eliminate background noise as much as possible. Speak slowly. If the trouble continues, try using the microphone on the Echo remote control.

Still having trouble? Try the Voice Training feature of the Echo app. On the left navigation panel, scroll toward the bottom and select **Voice Training**. The app will prompt you to read aloud 25 phrases which will help acquaint Echo with the unique cadence and peculiarities of your speech.

The Echo Remote Control Isn't Connecting

Confirm that the remote has a fresh set of AAA batteries installed. In the Echo app, tap **Settings** > **Pair remote**, then press and hold the remote's Play button for five seconds. You can only use one remote with your Echo.

Can't Connect to Bluetooth

Position your mobile device within 30 feet of your Echo. Turn on Bluetooth on your mobile device. Verify your mobile device is paired with your Echo. If not, say, **"Alexa, pair my [phone]."** From your mobile device's Bluetooth settings menu, manually select your Echo from the list of available devices.

Still having trouble? These these steps:

1. In the Echo app, go to **Settings** > **[The name of your Echo]** > **Bluetooth**.
2. Select **Remove** to wipe all paired devices.
3. Try pairing your Echo with your Bluetooth device again.
4. Unplug the power cord from your Echo for three seconds, then re-insert the power cord.

Forcing a Software Update

The Echo, like all modern digital devices, has a CPU at its core, which means that it runs software, which means that it needs updating.

According to Amazon, Alexa looks for updates every night, but if you want to force an update (for example, if Alexa is having trouble controlling a home device), just press the mute button on the top of the can and let it sit that way for at least 30 minutes.

7 ► SUMMARY

You will find both rave and so-so reviews of your Amazon Echo, as you will of any new product. And whether you will love or forget about your Echo depends on you and what needs it fills. Limited or not, the Amazon Echo is poised to become your home's smartphone hub, and now that Amazon has published an SDK (Software Developer's Kit), more uses will be in their way.

For now, if you're looking for a good wireless speaker that does a whole lot more than Jambox or other Bluetooth enabled speaker, you may be very pleased, even though the Echo isn't meant to move from room to room. If you like Echo's voice-activation feature, slim design, always-on capabilities, and streaming music feature, you may be very happy.

You may also find yourself developing a relationship with Alexa. How many other people in your life can you say, "Turn up the music," or "What's the weather," and get louder music or a weather forecast without a frown, ugh, or delay. If only your pal Alexa could take out the garbage.

In addition, you now have the first iteration of Alexa. Just like smartfones and tablets, newer versions will be capable of doing more, better and faster. Amazon has opened the software door so many more apps and capabilities are now being developed.

Want more? There are a lot of Echo sites to visit. Try http://www.lovemyecho.com for the latest tips, tricks, news and discussions.

Made in the USA
Coppell, TX
05 November 2026

11314457R00026